I0005797

9780692613177

Compilation
by
Josh Leitz
Margo Leitz

Illustrations
by
Margo Leitz

DoASeder.com

# Preface

It was an annual event growing up in my family to celebrate the Passover with aunts and uncles, cousins and family friends; a religious tradition that has become the most meaningful holy season for me. It is my desire to continue this tradition with my family and friends, a time of intimate fellowship, eating the special foods only offered at the seder, and reading about G-d's intervention in the lives of His people thousands of years ago, and being reminded that He does that for us today.

The traditional haggadah, which means "the telling" in Hebrew, is the special prayer book used on Passover. It tells the story of the Exodus, G-d delivering His people from Egyptian bondage by His servant Moses. This is the story of G-d's plan of redemption for mankind which foreshadows the ultimate work of Messiah laid out in the New Testament. This haggadah will include New Testament scripture to shed light on the symbols represented in the service.

With the help of my son Josh and his wife Kehau, we have compiled this haggadah, to be used by Christians and Jews. The format contains the traditional Jewish order and content, but adds New Testament revelation.

I do recommend that the service be facilitated by someone who grew up in a traditional Jewish home helping with the preparation of the traditional foods, adding the Hebrew to the prayers, and teaching the melodies to the songs.

Bringing one's own family traditions to the Passover Seder is encouraged to enrich the entire experience.

I pray that your Passovers will become family celebrations flavored with rich meaning and deepened insights into the word of G-d.

- Margo Leitz

# Introduction

Passover or Pesach is the first of seven appointed feasts of the L-rd, ordained by the L-rd, to commemorate the departure of the Hebrew nation from Egypt.

As commanded in the Torah,

> "You shall observe the Feast of Unleavened Bread; for seven days you are to eat unleavened bread, as I commanded you, at the appointed time in the month Abib, for in it you came out of Egypt. And they shall not appear before Me empty handed." Exodus 23:15

The Torah, the first five books of Moses, is the written word of G-d, and the instructions and rituals for the holidays were passed down in the oral law.

Every year in the spring, Jews around the world will prepare a seder as a memorial to the original Passover event, and in the same prescribed order given at Mt. Sinai over 3,000 years ago. It is important to G-d that the teachings and history of the Jewish people be preserved and passed down to all generations.

As we read through the Haggadah, you will notice the introduction of a dash in the spellings of G-d and L-rd. According to Jewish law and tradition, it was forbidden to erase or discard any written document with the names of our Creator, or even speak His Hebrew name Yod He Vav He. The word Jehovah is used by Christians to pronounce the four letters of the tetragrammaton, and the name Adonai is substituted when reading the Holy Scriptures or Torah. The true pronunciation of His Name has been lost. With great respect, we will reverence His holy name by continuing this tradition.

The symbolism in the seder meal will remind us that G-d remembered His people in bondage and He had a plan for their deliverance.

During the seder we drink four cups of wine, we ask the four questions and we speak of the four sons. The significance of 4 derives from the four expressions of redemption in G-d's promise to Moses:

"Therefore, say to the Israelites: 'I am the L-rd, and I will bring you out from under the yoke of the Egyptians. I will free you from being slaves to them, and I will redeem you with an outstretched arm and with mighty acts of judgment. I will take you as my own people, and I will be your G-d. Then you will know that I am the L-rd your G-d, who brought you out from under the yoke of the Egyptians."   Exodus 6:6-7

### The First Cup
The Cup of Sanctification - *"I will bring you"*
Our physical removal from the geographical boundaries of Egypt

### The Second Cup
The Cup of Deliverance - *"I will free you"*
Our delivery from Egyptian dominance

### The Third Cup
The Cup of Blessing / Redemption - *"I will redeem you"*
The elimination of any future threat of enslavement by the great judgments inflicted upon the Egyptians

### The Fourth Cup
The Cup of Acceptance / Elijah's Cup - *"I will take you"*
Our election as G-d's chosen people at Mount Sinai,
the purpose of the Exodus.

# Preparing for Passover

Removal of Leaven (chametz)

In anticipation of the Passover week, it is traditional for the home to be cleansed of all *chametz*, any foods containing yeast or leaven.

> "Seven days you shall remove leaven from your houses; for whoever eats anything leavened from the first day until the seventh day, that person shall be cut off from Israel."
> Exodus 12:15

Leaven is a symbol for sin, and is used throughout the Scriptures. Therefore, eating anything made with yeast is not allowed during this holiday. This commandment points to the New Covenant prophesized, and the coming Messiah. Stated in 1 Corinthians 5:7 concerning our personal lives:

> "Clean out the old leaven so that you may be a new lump, just as you are in fact unleavened. For Messiah our Passover has also been sacrificed."
> 1 Corinthians 5:7

# Table Setting

We raise the seder plate for all to see, and name the special items clockwise. The significance of each item will be discussed with the unfolding of the seder.

- Zeroa — shank bone, roasted lamb or chicken leg bone
- Charoset — a mixture of nuts, fruit, wine,    and honey
- Maror — bitter herbs, typically red or white horseradish
- Karpas — parsley or any other vegetable, such as potatoes
- Beitzah — egg, a roasted hard-boiled egg

Other items include:

- Holiday candles
- Covered plate, for three pieces of matzah.
- Bowl of salt water, for dipping
- Wine glasses
- Extra wine glass and place setting, for Elijah the Prophet
- Pillows, for each chair for reclining
- Cup and towel, for washing
- Haggadahs for each person

*Without the children watching, hide the afikoman, a broken piece of matzah, to be searched by the children later and then ransomed for money or a prize.*

# Seder   סדר

The seder is the meal celebrating Passover. Seder means order, and has a special order:

## Lighting of the Yom Tov   יום טוב
Blessing over the candles

## Kaddesh   קדש
Blessing of the first cup of wine, the cup of salavation

## Ur'Chatz   ורחץ
The leader washes his hands

## Karpas   כרפס
Dipping a vegetable in salt water and saying a blessing

## Yachatz   יחץ
Breaking the middle matzah, in two pieces, and hiding the larger half called the Afikomen

## Maggid   מגיד
Telling the story of Passover, asking the four questions, blessing of the second cup of wine

## Kos G'ulah   כוס גאולה
Blessing of the second cup of wine, the cup of plagues

## Rachtzah   רחצה
Washing our hands and saying blessing

## Motzi/Matzah   מוציא מצה
Saying the blessing for the matzah (bread)

## Maror מרור
Dipping the bitter herbs in charoset and saying the blessing

## Korech כורך
Eating a sandwich of matzah and bitter herbs

## Shulchan Orech שלחן עורך
Eating the festive meal

## Tzafun צפון
Eating the Afikomen, the hidden piece of matzah is found and brought back to the table, broken into pieces to be distributed to all

## Barech ברך
Blessing after the meal and the blessing of the third cup of wine, the cup of blessing

## Elijah אליהו
A child opens the door to see if the prophet is there, the one to precede the coming of Messiah

## Hallel הלל
Singing songs of praise

## Kos Hartza-ah כוס הרצאה
Blessing of the fourth cup of wine, the cup of acceptance

## Counting The Omer ספירת העומר
We count the days to the next "Feast of the L-rd", Shavuot (Pentacost)

## Nirtzah נרצה
Seder is completed

# Lighting the Yom Tov יום טוב

Holiday candles

Before the start of every Sabbath or Jewish holiday and before sunset, it is traditional for the women of the household to light two candles to welcome Shabbat or holy days:

ברוך אתה אדוני אלוהינו מלך העולם אשר

קדשנו במצותיו וצונו להדליק נר של יום טוב:

*Baruch atah Adonai Eloheinu Melech ha'olam asher kid'shanu b'mitzvotav v'tzivanu l'hadlik ner shel yom tov.*

Blessed are you, L-rd, our G-d, Sovereign of the Universe who has sanctified us with His commandments and commanded us to light the lights of this good day (festival lights).

8

# Kaddesh קדש

Blessing of the wine
The First Cup
The Cup of Sanctification

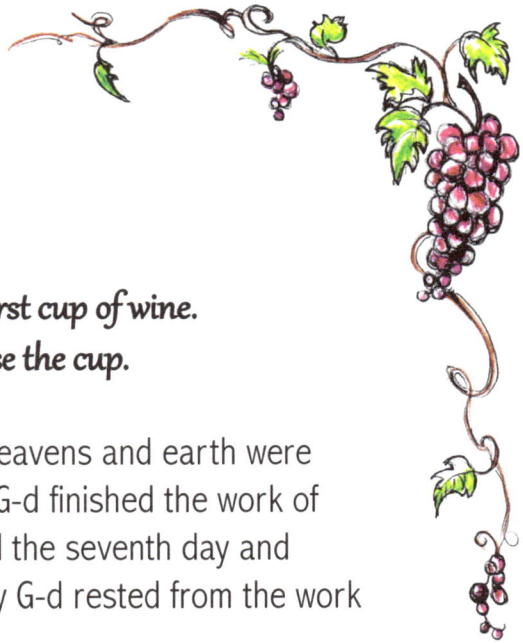

*Fill the first cup of wine.*
*Raise the cup.*

**LEADER**:  On the sixth day, the heavens and earth were completed.  On the seventh day, G-d finished the work of creation and rested.  G-d blessed the seventh day and called it holy, because on that day G-d rested from the work of creation.

ברוך אתה אדוני אלוהינו מלך העולם
בורא פרי הגפן:

*Baruch atah Adonai Elo-heinu Melech ha'olam*
*boreh p'ri hagafen.*

Blessed are You, L-rd our G-d, King of the Universe,
who creates the fruit of the vine.

**ALL**:  We praise You, Adonai our G-d, ruler of the universe who has made us holy through your mitzvoth (commandments) and lovingly given us Shabbat for rest and festivals for gladness.  You have given us Shabbat and this festival of matzot, celebrations of our freedom, a holy time to recall our going out of Egypt.  We praise You, Adonai, Who makes holy Shabbat, the people of Israel and the festivals.

9

*(If Passover lands on Saturday night, the Havdalah is added)*

ברוך אתה אדוני אלוהינו מלך העולם

בורא מאורי האש:

*Baruch atah Adonai, Eloheinu Melech ha'olam
bore me'orei ha'esh.*

Blessed are You, L-rd our G-d, King of the Universe,
Creator of the light of the fire.

ברוך אתה אדוני אלוהינו מלך העולם

שהחינו וקימנו והגיענו לזמן הזה:

*Baruch atah Adonai, Eloheinu Melech ha'olam
shehecheyanu, v'kiy'manu, v'higianu, lazman hazeh.*

Blessed are You, L-rd our G-d, King of the Universe,
who has kept us alive and well so that we can celebrate this
special time.

**LEADER**: This first cup speaks of the holiness or sanctification of the day of deliverance. In the New Testament believers are sanctified through the shed blood of Messiah.

> "How much more will the shed blood of Messiah, who through the eternal Spirit offered Himself without blemish to G-d, cleanse your conscience from dead works, to serve the living G-d." Hebrews 9:14

**ALL**: We offer a prayer of thanksgiving: We thank you L-rd for the cup of sanctification which speaks of setting us apart in Your holiness.

*The first cup of wine is drunk.*

# Urchatz ורחץ

The washing of the hands

**LEADER**: We will now prepare for the meal by washing our hands, symbolizing the sacredness of this occasion, and the purity of heart and hands that we are called to exhibit as G-d's people.

*The leader or head of the family*
*does the first hand washing.*

The New Testament speaks of Messiah at His last seder washing the feet of His disciples, demonstrating servanthood and complete humility.

"Now before the Passover Festival, Jesus realized that his hour had come to leave this world and return to the Father. Having loved his own who were in the world, he loved them to the end....Then he poured some water into a basin and began to wash the disciples' feet and to dry them with the towel that was tied around his waist." John 13:1-5

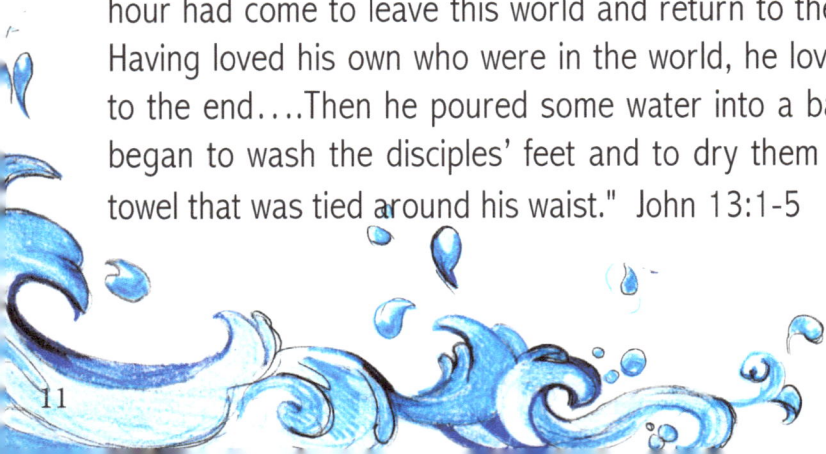

# Karpas כרפס

Parsley in salt water

*Dip a vegetable in salt water
and say the blessing:*

ברוך אתה אדוני אלוהינו מלך
העולם בורא פרי האדמה:

*Baruch atah Adonai Eloheinu Melech ha'olam
borei p'ri ha'adamah.*

Blessed are You, L-rd our G-d, Creator of the Universe, Who creates the fruit of the earth.

**ALL**: We are, duty bound to praise, thank, glorify, exalt, honor, bless and adore Him, who performed all these wonders for our fathers and for us. He brought us out of slavery into freedom, out of misery into happiness, out of mourning into rejoicing, out of darkness into His light, and out of bondage into redemption. Let us praise Him!

*Eat the vegetable.*

The karpas represents life and renewal. We dip it into salt water, which represents tears, and we eat it. The life as a slave is bitter and full of tears and hard labor. The karpas may also represent the hyssop, the plant that was dipped into the blood of the Passover lamb and applied to the doorposts of the houses in Egypt before the Exodus. We have new life in Messiah brought forth by His sacrifice on the cross.

# Yachatz יחץ
Dividing the middle Matzah

The leader takes three matzot and place into a matzot tash (a white, silk bag with three separate compartments, one for each matzah.) The middle piece is broken in half and the largest piece, the Afikomen, is set aside as the dessert matzah and wrapped in a white napkin to be eaten at the end of the meal. The smaller piece is returned to the seder plate.

*The seder plate is raised for all to see.*

**LEADER**:  This is the bread of affliction which our forefathers ate in the land of Egypt.

**ALL**:   Let all who are hungry come in and eat; let all who are in need join us as we celebrate the Passover feast. Now we celebrate here.  Next year may we be in the land of Israel.

*The tray with the matzot is moved aside.*

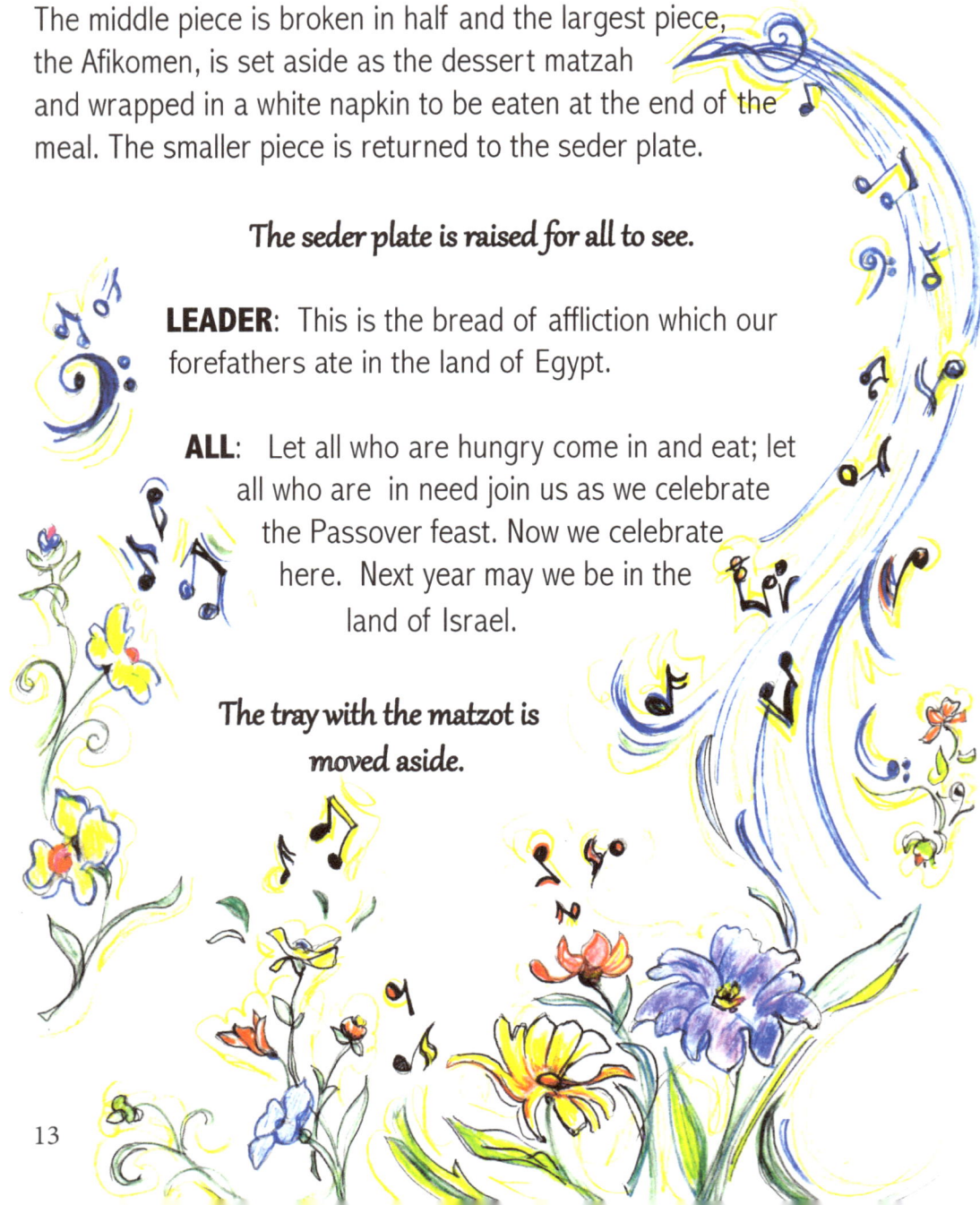

# Maggid  מגיד

The telling of the story of Passover

**LEADER**: Passover provides a yearly opportunity to teach our children G-d's plan of redemption. It is written in the Torah:

> You shall observe this service. And it will come about when your children will say to you, "What does this service mean to you?" that you shall say, "It is the Passover service to the L-rd." Exodus 12:25-27

To make sure that the children fulfill this Scripture, there are four questions that the youngest son is to ask on Passover.

*The youngest child asks or sings the*
*Four Questions on Passover.*

Why is this night different from all other nights?

א  On all other nights we eat bread or matzah; on this night why do we eat only matzah?

ב  On all other nights we eat all kinds of vegetables; on this night why do we eat only maror?

ג  On all other nights we not have to dip vegetables even once; on this night why do we dip them twice?

ד  On all other nights we eat our meals sitting any way we like; on this night, why do we lean on pillows?

# מַה נִּשְׁתַּנָּה הַלַּיְלָה הַזֶּה מִכָּל הַלֵּילוֹת

*Ma nishtanah ha-lailah ha-zeh mi-kol ha-leilot?*

**א**
שבכל הלילות אנו אוכלין חמץ ומצה
הלילה הזה כלו מצה:

*Sheb'chol haleilot anu ochlin chametz u'matzah, ha lailah hazeh kulo matzah.*

**ב**
שבכל הלילות אנו אוכלין שאר ירקות
הלילה הזה מרור:

*Sheb'chol haleilot anu ochlin she'ar yirakot, halailah hazeh maror.*

**ג**
שבכל הלילות אין אנו מטבילין אפילו פעם
אחת הלילה הזה שתי פעמים:

*Sheb'chol haleilot ein anu matbilin afilu pa'am echat, halailah hazeh sh'tei f'amim.*

**ד**
שבכל הלילות אנו אוכלין בין יושבין ובין
מסבין הלילה הזה כלנו מסבין:

*Sheb'chol haleilot anu ochlin bein yoshvin u'vein m'subin, halailah hazeh kulanu m'subin.*

## Translation

Why is this night different from all other nights?

1. On all other nights we eat leavened products and matzah, and on this night only matzah.
2. On all other nights we eat all vegetables, and on this night only bitter herbs.
3. On all other nights, we don't dip our food even once, and on this night we dip twice.
4. On all other nights we eat sitting or reclining, and on this night we only recline.

15

**LEADER**: "And you shall observe this event as an ordinance for you and your children forever.  And it will come about when you enter the land which the L-rd will give you, as He spoke, that you shall observe this service.  And it will come about when your children will say to you, 'What does this celebration mean to you?' That you shall say, 'It is a Passover sacrifice to the L-rd because He passed over the houses of the sons of Israel in Egypt when He smote the Egyptians, but delivered our homes.'  And the people bowed low and worshipped." Exodus 12:24-27

**ALL**:  We were Pharaoh's slaves in Egypt and the L-rd our G-d rescued us with a mighty hand and an outstretched arm. And if the L-rd, blessed be He, had not brought our forefathers out of Egypt, then we and our children and our children's children would still be slaves.

**LEADER**:  Our children have asked:  "Why do we eat only matzah?"

**ALL**:  We left Egypt in a hurry and there was no time for the bread to rise in our haste to leave Egypt.

**LEADER**:  Our children have asked:  "Why do we only eat bitter herbs?

**ALL**:  We must remember the bitterness of slavery.

**LEADER**:  Our children have asked:  "Why do we dip twice?"

**ALL**:  To remind us that the dipping of hyssop in the blood of the lamb and smeared on the lintel and two doorposts caused the angel of death to pass over the houses.

**LEADER**:  Our children have asked:  "Why do we recline at the table while eating?"

**ALL**:  We are no longer slaves serving taskmasters, but free at last.

We say a blessing:

ברוך המקום ברוך הוא: ברוך שנתן תורה לצמו
ישראל ברוך הוא:

*Baruch hamakom, baruch hu. Baruch shenatan torah le'amo
yisrael, baruch hu.*

Blessed be G-d Who is everywhere,
Blessed is He.
Blessed be G-d Who gave the Torah to the people of Israel.
Blessed is He.

## The Four Children

The Torah describes four children who ask
questions about the Exodus. Tradition teaches
that these verses refer to four different types of
children.

The **Wise** child asks, "What are the testimonies, and the statutes, and the judgments, that the L-rd our G-d has commanded us?"

The parents will say, " We were slaves to Pharaoh in Egypt; and the L-rd brought us out of Egypt with a mighty hand. The L-rd showed great and distressing signs and wonder before our eyes against Egypt, Pharaoh, and all his household." Deuteronomy 6:20-21

The **Wicked** child asks, "What does this Passover service mean to you!?"

He says `to you,' but not to him! By excluding himself, he reveals the motive of his heart, which was not right before G-d. You, therefore, blunt his teeth and say to him: "It is because of this that the L-rd did for me when I left Egypt"; `for me' - but not for him! If he had been there, he would not have been redeemed!"

The **Simple** child asks, "What is this seder service?"

The parent should answer, "With a mighty hand G-d brought us out of Egypt. Therefore, we commemorate our deliverance tonight through this seder."

And then there is a child **Who does not know how to ask**, you must initiate him, as it is said:

"You shall tell your child on that day, `It is because of this that the L-rd did for me when I left Egypt.'"

# The Passover Story

The Passover story really begins in Genesis. G-d created man, male and female and placed them in the garden in Eden. Adam and Eve enjoyed an intimate relationship with their Father G-d until an act of disobedience led to their fall from the Glory of G-d. In His great mercy, He covered them with skins and removed them from their original home so they would not live eternally in a state of corruption. The story of Passover is the story of redemption and restoration of a chosen people who would be called out from the nations to become kings and priests of the L-rd.

Many generations later, around 2000 BC, G-d spoke to Abraham, who would be called the father of many nations, to leave his home in Ur of the Chaldeans and go to a new land which He would show him, and He would make him a great nation and bless him. Abraham left the idol worshipping culture of his day and by faith, journeyed to this unknown land promised to him and his seed after him.

Abraham, with his wife Sarah and his nephew Lot came to the land of Canaan. In their old age, Isaac was born promised by G-d, then Jacob was born to Isaac, and to Jacob, twelve sons including Joseph, and a daughter. There was a great famine in the land, and Jacob spoke to his sons to leave Canaan and travel to Egypt to buy grain.
Genesis 12:1-4

Jacob loved G-d, and the L-rd changed his name to Israel (he is prince of EL). G-d called to Jacob and said:

> "I am EL, the G-d of your father; do not be afraid to go down to Egypt, for I will make you a great nation there. I will go down with you to Egypt, and I will also surely bring you up again; and Joseph's hand will close your eyes." Genesis 46:3-4

The Israelites grew to be a mighty nation in Egypt, and the Pharaoh became fearful they would become too numerous and join themselves to another nation and war against the Egyptians.

"So they appointed taskmasters over them to afflict them with hard labor. And they built for Pharaoh storage cities, Pithom and Ramses. But the more they afflicted them, the more they multiplied and the more they spread out, so that they were in dread of the sons of Israel. They made their lives bitter with hard labor in mortar and bricks and at all kinds of labor." Exodus 1:11-14

In order to stop the Israelites from multiplying, Pharaoh commanded all the male babies to be cast into the Nile. The parents of Moses placed him in a basket among the reeds in the Nile fearful that they could not hide their child any longer from death. It was Pharaoh's daughter that drew the child out of the water and he became her son.

Moses grew up in the household of Pharaoh but could not ignore the suffering of his people. In his attempt to defend one of his countrymen, he killed an Egyptian taskmaster, and had to flee for his life.

Forty years later tending sheep and living with the Midianites in the desert, he sees a sight worth investigating, "a bush was burning with fire, yet the bush was not consumed." Exodus 3:2

G-d calls to Moses out of the bush and says,

"I have surely seen the affliction of My people who are in Egypt, and have given heed to their cry because of their taskmasters, for I am aware of their sufferings. So I have come down to deliver them from the power of the Egyptians, and to bring them up from that land to a good and spacious land, to a land flowing with milk and honey..." Exodus 3:7-8

G-d sends Moses to Egypt with instructions to tell the people, "The G-d of your fathers has sent me to you, and His name is "I AM WHO I AM". Exodus 3:14 He is told to go to Pharaoh to warn him of the destruction to befall on Egypt if he refuses to let His people go.

Pharaoh's hard heartedness refuses to free the Israelites, and G-d unleashes the ten plagues on Egypt. After each plague, Pharaoh promises to release the people, but quickly recants to endure the next onslaught. It was after the tenth plague, the death of the firstborn, that Pharaoh allows the Israelites to leave the country.

The tenth plague called for the death of all the firstborn, the firstborn of the Israelites, the firstborn of every Egyptian, and every firstborn of the cattle.

## The L-rd redeems His people

"Now the L-rd said to Moses and Aaron in the land of Egypt: This month shall be the beginning for you; it is to be the first month of the year to you.

Speak to all the congregation of Israel saying, On the tenth of this month they are each to take according to their father's household a lamb for each household. Now if the household is too small for a lamb, then he and his neighbor nearest to his house are to take one according to the number of persons in them; according to what each man should eat you are to divide the lamb. Your lamb shall be an unblemished male a year old; you may take it from the sheep or the goats. And you shall keep it until the fourteenth day of the same month, then the whole assembly of the congregation of Israel is to kill it at twilight.

"Moreover, they shall take some of the blood and put it on the two doorposts and on the lintel of the houses in which they eat it. And

they shall eat the flesh that same night, roasted with fire, and they shall eat it with unleavened bread and bitter herbs. Do not eat any of it raw or boiled with water, but rather roasted with fire, both its head and its legs along with its entrails. And you shall not leave any of it over until morning, but whatever is left of it until morning, you shall burn with fire. Now you shall eat it in this manner: with your loins girded, your sandals on your feet, and your staff in your hand; and you shall eat it in haste — it is the L-rd's Passover. For I will go through the land of Egypt on that night and will strike down all the firstborn in the land of Egypt, both man and beast; and against all the gods of Egypt I will execute judgments — I am the L-rd. And the blood shall be a sign for you on the houses where you live; and when I see the blood I will pass over you and no plague will befall you to destroy you when I strike the land of Egypt.

"Then the sons of Israel went and did so; just as the L-rd had commandedMoses and Aaron, so they did. Now it came about at midnight that the L-rd struck all the firstborn in the land of Egypt, from the firstborn of the Pharaoh who sat on his throne to the firstborn of the captive who was in the dungeon, and all the firstborn cattle. And Pharaoh rose in the night, he and all his servants and all the Egyptians; and there was a great cry in Egypt, for there was no home where there was not someone dead. Then he called Moses and Aaron at night and said, "Rise up, get out from among my people, both you and the sons of Israel; and go, worship the L-rd as you have said." Exodus 12:1-13, 28-31

G-d's promise to Israel was kept in the covenant He swore to Abraham, "Know for certain that your descendants will be s trangers in a land that is not theirs, where they will be enslaved and oppressed for four hundred years. But I will also judge the nation whom they will serve; and afterward they will come out with great possessions." Genesis 15:13-14

The Passover story is a picture of the prophesied Messiah (Daniel 9:24) who would enter history and die on the very day of Passover 2,000 years ago. G-d's plan to redeem a people from original sin for himself is the deeper meaning of Passover. His free gift of salvation is for everyone who calls on the name of the L-rd.

"…Behold, the lamb of G-d who takes away the sin of the world." John 1:29

23

The L-rd G-d made a way for us to return to the garden in Eden in heaven, and to restore our original relationship with our Creator, by the sacrificial blood of Messiah Yeshua the Son of G-d. He delivered us from our own bondages in Egypt (this physical world), and sets us free to enjoy His abundant life forever.

# Kos G'ulah כוס גאולה

The Second Cup
Cup of Plagues or Cup of Deliverance

We fill this cup in remembering the joy of leaving Egypt.

*The second cup of wine is filled.*

Our joy is not complete because we remember that the Egyptians were also G-d's children who suffered and died under the rule of Pharaoh. We spill a drop of wine from the cup with our finger or spoon onto a plate as we say each plague:

| # | English | Heb. Trans. | Hebrew | Egyptian god | Reference |
|---|---------|-------------|--------|--------------|-----------|
| 1 | Water turned to blood | Dahm | דם | Osiris, Hapi | Ex 7:14 |
| 2 | Frogs cover the land | Tz'far-day-ah | צפרדע | Heket | Ex 8:1 |
| 3 | Lice | Ki-neem | כנים | Geb | Ex 8:16 |
| 4 | Swarms of flies | Ah-rov | ערוב | Uatchit | Ex 8:20 |
| 5 | Cattle disease | Dever | דבר | Apis, Hathor | Ex 9:1 |
| 6 | Boils | Sh'cheen | שחין | Isis | Ex 9:8 |
| 7 | Hail and fire | Barad | ברד | Nut | Ex 9:13 |
| 8 | Locusts | Ar-beh | ארבה | Seth | Ex 10:1-2 |
| 9 | Darkness | Cho-shech | חשך | Ra, Aten, Horus | Ex 10:21 |
| 10 | Death of the firstborn | Makat B'chorot | מכת בכורות | Judgement of Pharoah & Egypt | Ex 11:1 Ex 12:1 |

## CROSSING THE SEA, the story continues

[5]When the king of Egypt was told that the people had fled, Pharaoh and his servants had a change of heart toward the people, and they said, "What is this we have done, that we have let Israel go from serving us?" [6] So he made his chariot ready and took his people with him; [7] and he took six hundred select chariots, and all the other chariots of Egypt with officers over all of them. [8] The L-rd hardened the heart of Pharaoh, king of Egypt, and he chased after the sons of Israel as the sons of Israel were going out boldly. [9] Then the Egyptians chased after them with all the horses and chariots of Pharaoh, his horsemen and his army, and they overtook them camping by the sea, beside Pi-hahiroth, in front of Baal-zephon.

[10] As Pharaoh drew near, the sons of Israel looked, and behold, the Egyptians were marching after them, and they became very frightened; so the sons of Israel cried out to the L-rd. [11] Then they said to Moses, "Is it because there were no graves in Egypt that you have taken us away to die in the wilderness? Why have you dealt with us in this way, bringing us out of Egypt? [12] Is this not the word that we spoke to you in Egypt, saying, 'Leave us alone that we may serve the Egyptians'?

For it would have been better for us to serve the Egyptians than to die in the wilderness. [13]But Moses said to the people, "Do not fear! Take your stand and see the salvation of the L-rd which He will do for you today; for the Egyptians whom you have seen today, you will never see them again forever.

[21]Then Moses stretched out his hand over the sea, and the L-rd caused the sea to turn back by a strong east wind all night, and turned the sea into dry land, so the waters were divided....

²³The sons of Israel went through the midst of the sea with the Egyptians pursuing them...²⁶Then the L-rd said to Moses, "Stretch out your hand over the sea so that the waters may come back over the Egyptians, over their chariots and their horsemen." The waters covered the Egyptians and not one was left.

³¹When Israel saw the great power which the L-ord had used against the Egyptians, the people feared the L-ord, and they believed in the L-ord and in His servant Moses. Exodus 14:5-31

¹⁵:¹Then Moses and the sons of Israel sang this song to the L-ord, and said, "I will sing to the L-ord, for He is highly exalted; The horse and its rider He has hurled into the sea. ²"The L-rd is my strength and song, and He has become my salvation; This is my G-d, and I will praise Him; My father's G-d, and I will extol Him. Exodus 15:1-2

בכל דור ודור חייב אדם לראות את עצמו
כאילו הוא יצא ממצרים:

*B'chol dor vador chayav adam lirot et atsmo*
*k'ilu hu yatza mi'Mitzrayim.*

In each generation, everyone must think of himself or herself as having personally left Egypt.

27

# Dayenu דינו

## It Would Have Been Enough For Us!

Adonai has shown our people so many acts of kindness. For each one, we say, dayenu, meaning "that alone would have been enough, for that alone we are grateful."

**LEADER**: If G-d would have taken us out of Egypt and not executed judgment upon them, it would have been enough for us.

**ALL**: Dayenu.

**LEADER**: If He would have executed judgment upon them and not upon their idols, it would have been enough for us.

**ALL**: Dayenu.

**LEADER**: If He would have destroyed their idols, and not killed their firstborn, it would have been enough for us.

**ALL**: Dayenu.

**LEADER**: If He would have killed their firstborn, and not given us their wealth, it would have been enough for us.

**ALL**: Dayenu.

**LEADER**: If He would have given us their wealth, and not split the sea for us, it would have been enough for us.

**ALL**: Dayenu.

**LEADER**: If He would have split the sea for us, and not let us through it on dry land, it would have been enough for us.

**ALL**: Dayenu.

**LEADER**: If He would have let us through on dry land, and not drowned our enemies, it would have been enough for us.

**ALL**: Dayenu.

**LEADER**: If He would have drowned our enemies, and not provided for our needs in the desert for 40 years, it would have been enough for us.

**ALL**: Dayenu.

**LEADER**: But praise the L-rd! G-d provided permanent salvation through the sacrifice of the Messiah!

**ALL**: Dayenu! It is enough!

Hebrew Version:

אלו הוציאנו ממצרים דינו

*Ilu ho-tsi, ho-tsi-a-nu, Ho-tsi-anu mi-Mitz-ra-yim, Ho-tsi-anu mi-Mitz-ra-yim, Da-ye-nu*

*Da-da-ye-nu, Da-da-ye-nu, Da-da-ye-nu, Da-ye-nu Da-ye-nu*

# Matzah
Unleavened Bread

*The plate of matzah is raised for all to see.*

At the seder meal we eat matzah, unleavened
bread or bread without yeast, to remind us how the Israelites had to flee Egypt in haste, so that their bread did not have time to rise.  Another name for Passover is the Feast of Matzot.

> "And they baked the dough which they had brought out of Egypt into cakes of unleavened bread.  For it had not become leavened, since they were driven out of Egypt and could not delay, nor had they made provisions for themselves."
> Exodus 12:39

Three matzot were placed on the seder plate.  The number three is a symbol of unity:

### Unity of the fathers
Abraham, Isaac, and Jacob

### Unity of worship
The priests, the Levites, and the congregation

### Unity of the Trinity
Father, Son, HaRuach HaKodesh (the Holy Spirit)

The unleavened bread is a picture of Yeshua HaMeshiach.  It is simply made of pure flour and water without yeast, the symbol for sin.  The dough is flattened before it is baked, pierced and striped with a pointed tool to so not to bubble while baking.  The breaking of the matzah is a picture of the broken body of Messiah, broken and sacrificed for our redemption in Him.

Old Testament prophetic scriptures point to Messiah:

"They pierced my hands and my feet. I can count all my bones. " Psalms 22:16

"They will look on me who they have pierced; they will mourn for him, as one mourns for an only son, and they will weep bitterly over him, like the bitter weeping over a firstborn." Zechariah 12:10

"He was wounded for our transgressions, he was bruised for our iniquities; the chastisement of our peace was upon him; and with his stripes we are healed." Isaiah 53:5

*Each person receives broken pieces of matzah.*

# Zeroa
The Bone

*Point to the lamb bone*

The roasted shank bone is called the Pesach (Passover). It is the symbol for the lamb that was sacrificed and eaten on the night of the Passover, and by applying the blood on the lintel and doorposts of their houses, the angel of death "passed over" the Israelites and spared their firstborn.

"When I see the blood, I will pass over you." Exodus 12:13

"By faith he (Moses) kept the Passover and the sprinkling of the blood, so that he who destroyed the firstborn might not touch them." Hebrews 11:28

# Charoset
The Apple Mixture

The Charoset is a symbol for the mud and straw needed to make the bricks and mortar to build Pharaoh's cities. It is a sweet mixture made with chopped apples, chopped walnuts, honey, cinnamon and wine or grape juice.

# Marror
Bitter Herbs

We eat the bitter herbs on Passover. Horseradish is usually served to remind us of the bitterness of slavery and the tears brought on by harsh living.

### *The plate of marror is pass around.*

Before we were redeemed, sin made our life bitter and miserable.

> "And He brought us forth from there, in order to bring us in, that He might give us the land which He swore unto our ancestors." Deuteronomy 6:23

We personally come to identify with the redemption provided by the Messiah, with His death, His burial and His resurrection.

# Karpas
Vegetable

Parsley is a symbol of life. We dip the parsley into a bowl of salt water, a symbol of tears, and then eaten. We remember that life in bondage is full of tears.

# Betza
The Egg

The egg is a symbol of mourning, and was added to the seder after the Temple in Jerusalem was destroyed by the Romans in 70 AD.  The Temple was the place where the Jewish priests offered the animal sacrifices for the Jewish people all year and especially on Yom Kippor.  The sacrificial system is no longer available and so sacrifices are no longer offered.  The roasted egg is also a symbol of new life and hope, and points to the grace of G-d and new life in Messiah.

### Raise the cup of wine.

We praise You, Adonai our G-d, Ruler of the Universe, Who has freed us and our ancestors from Egypt and brought us here this night to eat matzah and maror.  Adonai, our G-d and G-d of our ancestors, help us celebrate future holidays and festivals in peace and in joy.  Then we will thank You with a new song.

ברוך אתה אדוני גאל ישראל:

*Baruch atah Adonai, ga'al Yisrael.*

We praise You, Adonai our G-d, Who has freed the people of Israel.

ברוך אתה אדוני אלוהינו מלך העולם
בורא פרי הגפן:

*Baruch atah Adonai Elo-heinu Melech ha'olam*
*boreh p'ri hagafen.*

We praise You, Adonai our G-d, Ruler of the Universe, Who creates the fruit of the vine.

### The second cup of wine, The Cup of Deliverence, is now drunk.

# Rachtzah רחצה
## Second Ritual Handwashing

Pour water from a cup once on each hand over a sink or basin hands, this time with a blessing, to prepare for the eating of the matzah. We wash our hands to demonstrate our sanctification as G-d's people and as an act of purification so we may approach G-d with a pure heart and clean hands.

ברוך אתה אדוני אלוהינו מלך העולם אשר
קדשנו במצותיו וצונו על נטילת ידים:

*Baruch atah Adonai Eloheinu Melech ha'olam asher kid'shanu b'mitzvotav v'tzivanu al nitilat yadayim.*

Blessed are You, L-rd our G-d, King of the Universe, Who has sanctified us with His laws and commands us to wash our hands.

# Motzi/Matzah מוציא מצה
## Blessing before the Seder Meal

### *The broken pieces of matzah are distributed.*

ברוך אתה אדוני אלוהינו מלך העולם
המוציא לחם מן הארץ:

*Baruch atah Adonai Eloheinu Melech ha'olam hamotzi lechem min ha'aretz.*

Blessed are You, L-rd our G-d, King of the Universe, who brings bread from the earth.

34

ברוך אתה אדוני אלוהינו מלך העולם
אשר קדשנו במצותיו וצונו על אכילת
מצה:

*Baruch atah Adonai Eloheinu Melech ha'olam,*
*asher kid'shanu b'mitzvotav v'tzivanu al achilat matzah.*

Blessed are You, L-rd our G-d, King of the Universe, who has sanctified us with His laws and commanded us to eat matzah.

# Maror מרור

The blessing for the Maror

ברוך אתה אדוני אלוהינו מלך העולם
אשר קדשנו במצותיו וצונו על אכילת
מרור:

*Baruch atah Adonai Eloheinu Melech ha'olam,*
*asher kid'shanu b'mitzvotav v'tzivanu al achilat maror.*

Blessed are You, L-rd our G-d, King of the Universe, who has sanctified us with His laws and commanded us to eat bitter herbs.

# Korech כורך

Matzah, charoset and bitter herb sandwich

Each person makes a sandwich placing the charoset and maror together between two broken pieces of matzah and eat. The combination of bitterness and sweetness reminds us that although sin is harsh and miserable, we have the sweetness of redemption when we believe in Messiah.

# Shulchan Orech שלחן עורך

Eating of the festival meal

*We now eat and continue reading after the Passover meal.*
*You may drink wine between the second and third cups.*

# Tzafun צפון

Eating of the afikomen

*After the Passover meal, the children may now search to find the*
*afikoman. Once found, it is given to the "Father" and ransomed for*
*money or a prize.*

This is the middle broken piece of matzah that was hidden away earlier
in the evening.  It symbolizes the breaking of the body of the Son of
G-d, unleavened, striped, pierced, wrapped up and hidden.

As Messiah broke the matzah and gave it to His disciples,

> "Take, eat; this is My body which is given for you; do this in
> remembrance of Me." Luke 22:19

We too, participate in communion with Him by celebrating the Passover.

New Testament revelation adds to the meaning of this bread  in this
scripture when Messiah says to His disciples,

> "... it is not Moses who has given you the bread out of
> heaven, but it is My Father who gives you the true bread out
> of heaven. For the bread of G-d is that which comes down out

of heaven, and gives life to the world. They said therefore to Him, L-rd, evermore give us this bread. Yeshua said to them, I am the bread of life; he who comes to Me shall not hunger, and he who believes in Me shall never thirst." John 6:32-35

"I am the bread of life. Your fathers ate the manna in the wilderness, and they died. This is the bread which comes down out of heaven, so that one may eat of it and not die. I am the living bread that came down out of heaven; if anyone eats of this bread, he shall live forever; and the bread also which I shall give for the life of the world is My flesh."
John 6:48-51

"The L-rd's Supper" was the Passover of the New Covenant. We have communion and fellowship, as the body of believers, with the L-rd Himself (1 Corinthians 10:16-17).

# Barech ברך

Blessing after the Meal
The Third Cup of Redemption

*The third cup of wine is poured.*
*Raise the cup and we say the blessing after the meal.*

Blessed are You, L-rd our G-d, King of the Universe, who sustains the entire world with goodness, grace, loving kindness, and compassion. He gives bread to all, for His grace is everlasting. And in His great goodness we have never lacked anything and we will never be deprived of food for the sake of His great name. For He is G-d who provides for all and does good for all and prepares food for all His creatures that He created. Blessed are You, L-rd, who provides for all life.

עושה שלום במרומיו הוא יעשה שלום
עלינו ועל כל ישראל ואמרו אמן

*Oseh Shalom Bim-romav Hu Yaaseh Shalom Aleinu Ve-al Kol
Yisrael Ve-Imru Amen*

May the Holy One, Who makes peace in the Heavens, make
peace for us, for Israel, and for all the world.  Amen.

## We say the blessing over the Cup of Redemption:

ברוך אתה אדוני אלוהינו מלך
העולם בורא פרי הגפן:

*Baruch Ata Adonai Eloheinu Melech ha'olam
borei p'ri hagafen.*

Blessed are You,  Adonai our G-d, Ruler of the Universe who
creates the fruit of the vine.

## The third cup is now drunk.

The third cup symbolizes our redemption out of Egypt.  As this cup is
fulfilled in the New Covenant, with Yeshua saying during the seder,

> "This cup which is poured out for you is the new covenant in
> My blood." Luke 22:20

The Old Testament prophesized,

> " Behold, the days are coming, saith the L-rd, when I will make
> a new covenant with the house of Israel and with the house of
> Judah." Jeremiah 31:31

# Welcoming Elijah אליהו

The Fourth Cup
The Cup of Acceptance

*The fourth cup is poured and the door is opened.*

The cup of acceptance is also referred to as Elijah's cup.  We open the door looking for Elijah the prophet, Eliyahu Hanavi who will announce the coming of Messiah.  Tradition has us set a place setting for the prophet to honor his presence. Scripture tells us that he did not die, but was taken up to heaven in a "whirlwind" by almighty G-d. (2 Kings 2:1).

We now know from New Testament revelation that Elijah was the forerunner of John the Baptist who proclaimed the coming of the Messiah, when he said,

> "Repent for the kingdom of the heavens is at hand. For this is the one referred to by Isaiah the prophet saying 'The voice of one crying in the wilderness, make ready the way of the L-rd, make His paths straight.'" (Mathew 3:2-3, Isaiah 40:3)

# Hallel הלל

Psalms of Praise (Psalms 113, 114)

**LEADER**: Praise the L-rd!

**ALL**: Praise, O servants of the L-rd, praise the name of the L-rd.

**LEADER**: Let the name of the L-rd be praised, both now and forever more.

**ALL**: From the rising of the sun to the place where it sets, the name of the L-rd is to be praised.

**LEADER**: The L-rd is exalted over all the nations, His glory above the heavens.

**ALL**: Who is like the L-rd our G-d, the One who sits enthroned on high, who stoops down to look on the heavens and the earth?

**LEADER**: He raises the poor from the dust and lifts the needy from the ash heap; He seats them with princes, with the princes of their people.

**ALL**: He settles the barren woman in her home as a happy mother of children.

**LEADER**: Praise the L-rd!

**ALL**: When Israel came out of Egypt, the house of Jacob from a people of foreign tongue, Judah became G-d's sanctuary, Israel his domain.

**LEADER**: The sea looked and fled, the Jordan turned back; the mountains skipped like rams, and the hills like lambs.

**ALL**: Why was it, O sea, that you fled, O Jordan, that you turned back, you mountains that you skipped like rams, you hills like lambs?

**LEADER**: Tremble, O earth at the presence of the L-rd, at the presence of the G-d of Jacob, who turned the rock into a pool, the hard rock into springs of water.

**ALL**: Blessed are You O L-rd our G-d, King of the universe, Creator of the fruit of the vine.

*Additional reading of the Psalms 115-118*

# Kos Hartza-ah כוס הרצאה

The Fourth Cup
The Cup of Acceptance

The Fourth cup represents "I will take you to me for a people." It reminds us that G-d accepts those whom He has chosen and saved by grace.

### We raise our cup and say the blessing:

ברוך אתה אדוני אלוהינו מלך העולם
בורא פרי הגפן:

*Baruch atah Adonai Eloheinu Melech ha'olam
borei p'ri hagafen.*

Blessed are You, Adonai our G-d, Ruler of the Universe who creates the fruit of the vine.

### We drink the final cup.

# Counting the Omer  ספירת העומר

The celebration of the Passover is also linked to the onset of the barley harvest. On the second day of Passover, an offering of one omer, or sheaf of barley, was brought to the temple, and the counting of the omer began. The 50th day from Passover ushered in the beginning of the wheat harvest which coincides with the 49 days it took the Israelites to reach Mt. Sinai after the Exodus from Egypt.

Shavuot, which means seven sevens in Hebrew, is the holiday following Passover exactly 49 days after the first day of Passover, and commemorates the giving of the Torah on Mt. Sinai. The Greek word for Shavuot is Pentacost, meaning 50, and exactly on this day after the death of Messiah on the cross, G-d poured out His Holy Spirit, HaRuach HaKodesh, on the new believers in Yeshua HaMeshiach.

The Holy Scriptures or the Old Testament is the inspired word of G-d, and His plan for salvation is specifically and completely fulfilled in the New Testament by the coming of Messiah and His death on a tree. Yeshua died on the very day the Jews were celebrating the Passover.

His redemption of his people from a fallen state to restored glory was always in the heart of the Father. Passover is a picture from slavery to deliverance and on Shavuot we received the power of the Holy Spirit.

ברוך אתה אדוני אלוהינו מלך העולם
אשר קדשנו במצותיו וצונו על ספירת
העומר: היום יום אחד לעומר:

*Baruch atah Adonai Eloheinu Melech ha'olam asher kid'shanu b'mitzvotav v'tzivanu al s'firat ha'omer. Hayom yom echad la'omer.*

Blessed are You, Adonai our G-d, Ruler of the Universe, who makes us holy by Your mistzvot and commands us to count the Omer. Today is the first day of the Omer.

# Nirtzah נרצה
Completing the Seder

**LEADER**: The Passover seder is now complete, even as our salvation and redemption are complete.

It is a blessing to celebrate the Passover. May we be granted the blessing of celebrating Pesach for many years to come. The Holy One, who dwells in our hearts, raise up your people with love and lead us to Zion in joyful singing.

לשנה הבאה בירושלים
Lashanah haba'ah b'Yerushalayim!
**ALL: Next year in Jerusalem!**